# Cambridge ICT Starters

# On Track Stage 2

Third Edition

Jill Jesson and Graham Peacock

**CAMBRIDGE**
UNIVERSITY PRESS

# CAMBRIDGE
## UNIVERSITY PRESS

University Printing House, Cambridge CB2 8BS, United Kingdom

Cambridge University Press is part of the University of Cambridge.

It furthers the University's mission by disseminating knowledge in the pursuit of education, learning and research at the highest international levels of excellence.

Information on this title: education.cambridge.org

© Cambridge University Press 2013

First published 2003
Second edition 2005
Third edition 2013
4th printing 2015

Printed in Dubai by Oriental Press

*A catalogue record for this publication is available from the British Library*

ISBN 978-1-107-62515-0 Paperback

Additional resources for this publication at www.cambridgeindia.org

Cambridge University Press has no responsibility for the persistence or accuracy of URLs for external or third-party internet websites referred to in this publication, and does not guarantee that any content on such websites is, or will remain, accurate or appropriate. Information regarding prices, travel timetables, and other factual information given in this work is correct at the time of first printing but Cambridge University Press does not guarantee the accuracy of such information thereafter.

..............................................................................................

..............................................................................................

Every effort has been made to trace the owners of copyright material included in this book. The publishers would be grateful for any omissions brought to their notice for acknowledgement in future editions of the book.

# Introduction

*Cambridge ICT Starters: On Track, Stage 2* has been written to support learners who are following the Cambridge ICT Starters syllabus. It follows the syllabus closely and provides full coverage of all the modules. The sections of the book correspond to the modules and follow the order in which the modules appear in the syllabus. The book demonstrates how to design, correct and evaluate control system; build website with links and images; understand and design networks; and produce video and animation, incorporating audio effects.

The book provides learners and their helpers with:

*   examples of activities to do
*   exercises for practice
*   instruction in using their computers
*   optional extension and challenge activities

It is designed for use in the classroom with coaching from trained teachers. Where possible the work has been set in real situations where the computer will be of direct use. The activities are fairly sophisticated yet simple enough to be followed by adults as well as children!

Some exercises require the learners to open prepared files for editing. These files are available to teachers on www.cambridgeindia.org website. The website provides useful graphics and templates for creating pictograms. Some pictures and text files are also included to help young learners so that they can learn editing without first creating the files required.

The activities in this book use Windows 7, Microsoft Office 2007 software, Paint, Wikipedia, Microsoft Outlook Express 2007, MSWLogo and Windows Movie Maker. However, the syllabus does not specify any particular type of software in order to meet the learning objectives.

Please note that when learners view the screen shots contained in this book on their computer screens, all the type will be clearly legible.

# Contents

## ON TRACK: Stage 2

## Module 5 Control for a Purpose

| | | |
|---|---|---|
| 5.1 | Control devices | 2 |
| 5.2 | Flowcharts | 3 |
| 5.3 | Creating a working module | 4 |
| 5.4 | Looping | 5 |
| 5.5 | Input switch | 6 |
| 5.6 | Double sets of traffic lights | 7 |
| 5.7 | Using subroutines | 10 |
| 5.8 | Subroutines | 11 |
| 5.9 | Using a motor output | 13 |
| 5.10 | Greenhouse | 16 |
| 5.11 | Using variables | 18 |
| | *Optional extension and challenge activities* | 22 |

## Module 6 Website Design for a Purpose

| | | |
|---|---|---|
| 6.1 | Designing a website | 25 |
| 6.2 | Microsoft Expression | 26 |
| 6.3 | Creating web pages | 27 |
| 6.4 | Creating hyperlinks | 31 |
| 6.5 | Inserting images | 33 |
| 6.6 | Navigation menu | 35 |
| 6.7 | Refinements | 36 |
| 6.8 | HTML Code | 37 |
| | *Optional extension and challenge activities* | 38 |

## Module 7 Networks for a Purpose

| | | |
|---|---|---|
| 7.1 | Introduction to networks | 40 |
| 7.2 | Management issues | 45 |
| 7.3 | Assignment 1 | 46 |
| 7.4 | Assignment 2 | 49 |
| | *Optional extension and challenge activities* | 52 |

## Module 8 Video or Animation for a Purpose

| | | |
|---|---|---|
| 8.1 | Animation | 54 |
| 8.2 | Creating animation | 56 |
| 8.3 | Drafting | 58 |
| 8.4 | Video | 63 |
| 8.5 | Creating source clips | 64 |
| 8.6 | Editing video | 65 |
| 8.7 | Transition | 66 |
| 8.8 | Adding audio files | 67 |
| 8.9 | Narration | 68 |
| 8.10 | Titles and credits | 70 |
| 8.11 | Other titles | 71 |
| 8.12 | The final movie | 72 |
| 8.13 | Assignment | 73 |
| | *Optional extension and challenge activities* | 75 |

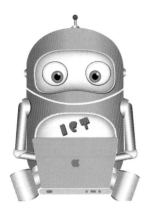

# Module 5
# Control for a Purpose

## Learning Objectives

| | Student is able to: | Pass/Merit |
|---|---|---|
| 1 | Design a control system | P |
| 2 | Build a sequence of events to activate multiple devices concurrently | P |
| 3 | Correct and improve procedures | M |
| 4 | Evaluate the system, identifying limitations | M |

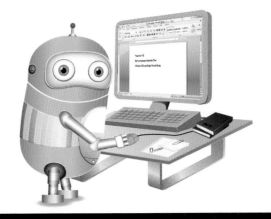

# 5.1 Control devices

## Control devices

- Examples of control devices:
  - fire alarm
  - traffic light
  - greenhouse
  - car-park barriers
  - burglar alarm
  - fridge-cooling system.

- Name 2 more common control systems or control devices:

  _____

  _____

## Inputs and outputs

- Each control device is set to receive inputs directly or through sensors.
- The device will then process according to the inputs and the conditions set.
- The reaction is then reflected in the outputs.

- Examples of inputs: microphones, switches, sensors that detect changes, TV aerials, sound detectors and light detectors.
- Examples of processors: amplifiers, decision-making circuits, counters, timers.
- Examples of outputs: light bulbs, LEDs, loudspeakers, motors.

## Identifying the devices

- Identify the input, processor and output devices of each system below (the first one is given as an example):
  - Fire alarm
    - Input: heat sensor
    - Processor: decision-making circuit
    - Output: sound (loudspeaker)
  - Traffic light
    - Input:
    - Processor:
    - Output:
  - Greenhouse
    - Input:
    - Processor:
    - Output:
  - Car-park barriers
    - Input:
    - Processor:
    - Output:

  - Burglar alarm
    - Input:
    - Processor:
    - Output:
  - Fridge-cooling system
    - Input:
    - Processor:
    - Output:

- Fill in the two control-device or control-system examples that you gave above:

  - _____
    - Input:
    - Processor:
    - Output:

  - _____
    - Input:
    - Processor:
    - Output:

## What are flowcharts?

- A process or work procedure can be illustrated by using flowcharts or graphical representations.
- Each step in a process is represented by a symbolic shape.
- The flow of the process is indicated by arrows connecting the symbols.
- Flowcharts are useful for displaying how a process functions or could ideally function.

- Flowcharts can help you see whether the steps of a process are logical.
- They can be used to uncover problems or miscommunications and to develop a common base of knowledge about a process.
- Flow-charting a process helps to avoid redundancies, delays, dead ends and indirect paths that would otherwise remain unnoticed or ignored.

## Basic symbols

**Oval**

- An oval indicates both the starting point and the ending point of the process.

**Box**

- A box represents an individual step or activity in the process.

**→ Flow line**

- This indicates the direction flow of the process.

**Box**

- A box with 2 side margins represents a subroutine.

**Circle**

- A circle indicates that a particular step is connected within the page. A numerical value placed in the circle indicates the sequence continuation.

 **Diamond**

- A diamond shows a decision point, such as yes/no or go/no-go. Each path emerging from the diamond must be labelled with one of the possible answers.

**Rhombus**

- A rhombus shows input or output devices.

## Examples of flowcharts

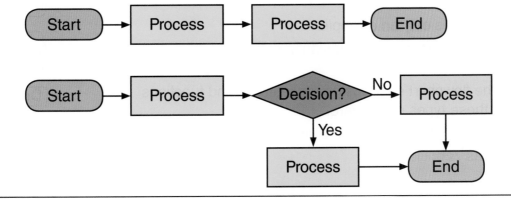

# 5.3 Creating a working module

## Design

- Design is the first of the 5 criteria for success in creating working module:
  - design
  - create
  - test
  - change
  - evaluate.
- Identify the function of the system, the inputs and the outputs.

- Collect evidence at each stage.
- Well-planned modules make it easier to test, change and evaluate the system.

*Failing to plan is planning to fail!*

## Zebra-crossing system

- Basically the system works as below:
  - The system turns on the light for the pedestrian to cross.
  - The light stays on for a few seconds.
  - The system turns off the light.
- The following shows the planning for creating the system.

| Description of the event in ordinary words | Control words | Flowchart symbol |
|---|---|---|
| Begin the system. | Start | Start |
| Turn on the light. | Turn on Output 1 | Input / Output |
| Let the light stay on for 5 seconds. | Delay 5 | Process |
| Turn off the light. | Turn off Output 1 | Input / Output |
| Stop the system. | Stop | Stop |

## Flowchart

- Draw the flowchart.
- The flowchart shown is only an example.
- Test the flowchart with appropriate simulation software such as Flowol or Learn & Go.
- You can draw the flowchart easily using the features and functions that come with these types of software.
- Software with special mimics makes the simulation more interesting.
- Save your work as zebra1.

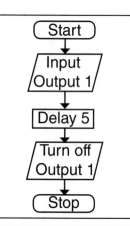

## Looping and blinking

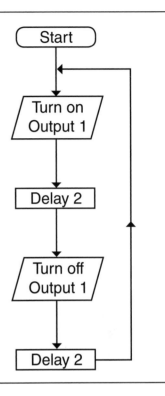

- The previous system stops until it is activated again.
- We can make the system blink by adding another delay and repeating the process.
- After the system is switched on, it will immediately trigger the light.
- The first delay will determine the duration for the light to stay on.
- The light is then turned off.
- The next delay will then determine the duration for the light to stay off.
- The loop – the line that leads the way back to the starting point – will repeat the whole system from the beginning.
- Make changes to your first flowchart.
- Test the new system again.
- Save your work as zebra2.

## The lighthouse

- The blinking effect can be applied to a lighthouse.
- Simultaneously, the lighthouse can also give a second output: the buzzer.

| Description of the event in ordinary words | Control words | Flowchart symbol |
|---|---|---|
| Begin the system. | Start | Start |
| Turn on the light and the buzzer. | Turn on output 1 and Output 2 | Input Output |
| Let the light and buzzer stay on for 5 seconds. | Delay 5 | Process |
| Turn off the light and the buzzer. | Turn off Output 1 and Output 2 | Input Output |
| Let the light stay on for 5 seconds. | Delay 5 | Process |
| Repeat the system. | Loop | (Lead the arrow back to the first Input/ Output box) |

## Multiple inputs and outputs

- Construct the flowchart.
- Some simulation software allows more than 2 inputs or outputs to be listed in the same symbol. (Check the manual for your software.)
- The inputs or outputs will be executed at the same time.
- Test your system.
- Save your work as lighthouse1.

Lighthouse

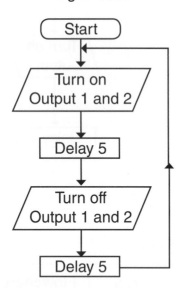

## Input and decision

- The brightness (sun/moon) can be used as an input for deciding whether the internal light of the lighthouse needs to be switched on or not.
- If it is bright (sun), the decision will lead to switching the output (internal light) off.
- If it is dim (moon), the decision will lead to switching the output (internal light) on.
- Test your system.
- Save your work as lighthouse2.

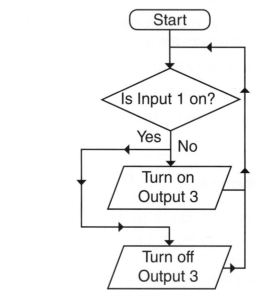

## Traffic lights

- At the start, the red light is switched on and stays on for 5 seconds.
- The green light is then switched on at the same time as the red light is switched off. The light stays on for another 5 seconds.
- The green light is then switched off while the yellow light is switched on simultaneously.
- The yellow light is allowed to stay on for 3 seconds before it is switched off while the red light is switched on. The process is then repeated.
- Based on the description above, construct the flowchart based on the contents of the table on the next page.

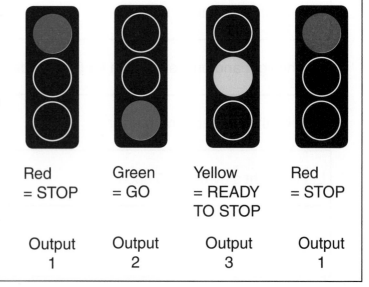

| Red<br>= STOP | Green<br>= GO | Yellow<br>= READY<br>TO STOP | Red<br>= STOP |
| --- | --- | --- | --- |
| Output<br>1 | Output<br>2 | Output<br>3 | Output<br>1 |

### Traffic lights

- Make a flowchart of the system indicated by the table.

| Description of the event in ordinary words | Control words | Flowchart symbol |
|---|---|---|
| Begin the system. | Start | Start |
| Turn on the red light. | Turn on output 1 | Input Output |
| Let the red light stay on for 5 seconds. | Delay 5 | Process |
| Turn off the red light and turn on the green light. | Turn off Output 1 and turn on Output 2 | Input Output |
| Let the light stay on for 5 seconds. | Delay 5 | Process |
| Turn off the green light and turn on the yellow light. | Turn off Output 2 and turn on Output 3 | Input Output |
| Let the light stay on for 3 seconds. | Delay 3 | Process |
| Repeat the system. | Loop | (Lead the arrow back to the first Input/ Output box) |

### Flowchart

- Use the simulation software to draw your flowchart.

- Print the flowchart and glue it in the space on the right.

- Test the system with your software, observe the limitations and compare it with a real-life situation. (Note: the suggested system may be different from the system in your country. You are free to make the necessary changes.)

- Save your work as traffic1.

*Glue your printed flowchart here!*

## Traffic lights at crossroads

- Two different sets of traffic lights are needed at the crossroads junction.
- The two sets of traffic lights must work with reference to each other.

| Output | Description | Function |
|--------|-------------|----------|
| Output 1 | Red 1 | Stop |
| Output 2 | Green 1 | Go |
| Output 3 | Yellow 1 | Wait |
| Output 4 | Red 2 | Stop |
| Output 5 | Green 2 | Go |
| Output 6 | Yellow 2 | Wait |

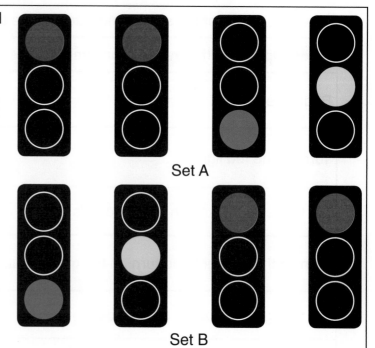

Set A

Set B

## Flowchart

- Complete the following table for creating the flowchart of a set of traffic lights.

| Description of the event in ordinary words | Control words | Flowchart symbol |
|--------------------------------------------|---------------|------------------|
| Begin the system. | Start | ( Start ) |
| Turn on the red light of set A. Turn on the green light of set B. | Turn on Output 1 and Output 5 | Input / Output |
| Let the red light stay on for 5 seconds. | Delay 5 | Process |
| Turn off the green light and turn on the yellow light of set B. The red light of set A should stay on. | | Input / Output |
| Let the light stay on for 3 seconds. | | Process |
| Turn off the yellow light and turn_____ _____ _____ light of set_____. Turn on the _____ light of set A. | | Input / Output |
| Let the light stay on for 5 seconds. | | Process |
| Turn off the _____ light and turn on the _____ light of set _____. The red light of set _____ should stay on. | | Input / Output |

# Flowchart (continued)

- Continue to complete the following table for creating the flowchart of a set of traffic lights.

| Description of the event in ordinary words | Control words | Flowchart symbol |
|---|---|---|
| Let the light stay on for 3 seconds. | Delay 3 | |
| Turn off yellow light and turn _____ _____ _____ light of set _____. Turn on the _____ light of set B. | Turn off Output 3. Turn on Output 1 and Output 6. | |
| Repeat the system. | Loop | |

- Save your work as traffic2.
- Test your system with simulation software.

# Evaluation

- Compare the system with a real-life system and discuss what possible changes you should make to improve the system.

  (Hints: 1. Compare the time delay of the system with the real-life system. Is the time delay long enough in terms of safety?

  2. In the system, the light turns green immediately after the red light is turned off. Is this safe? If not, what can be done about it?

  3. What limitations are there in this system? What will happen if there is a power failure?

  4. What will happen if one or more of the bulbs burn out?)

  ...........................................................................................................................................

  ...........................................................................................................................................

  ...........................................................................................................................................

  ...........................................................................................................................................

  ...........................................................................................................................................

  ...........................................................................................................................................

  ...........................................................................................................................................

  ...........................................................................................................................................

- Save your flowchart as traffic3.
- Re-set your flowchart using the software and make further changes needed.

## Pedestrian crossing

- The pedestrian-crossing system will be activated when it receives input from the pedestrian who wishes to cross the road.

- Here is a list of the input and outputs that are used:

| Input | Description |
|-------|-------------|
| Input 1 | Signal from pedestrian |

| Output | Description |
|--------|-------------|
| Output 1 | Red light – stops vehicles |
| Output 2 | Yellow light – warns vehicles to get ready to stop |
| Output 3 | Green light – safe for vehicles to continue |
| Output 4 | Red light – stops pedestrian from crossing |
| Output 5 | Green light – pedestrian safe to cross |

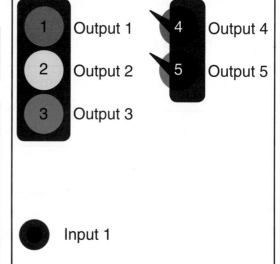

## Subroutines

- The system may need a long flowchart.
- You can always break down the flowchart into subroutines.
- You can then command them from a main routine.
- Some software may need to create the subroutine first.
- A subroutine starts with Sub. You can then give it a name.
- Use the table below to plan for a subroutine to stop the vehicle.
- Name the subroutine Sub 1(stop).

| Description of the event in ordinary words | Control words | Flowchart symbol |
|---------------------------------------------|---------------|------------------|
| Begin the subroutine. | Sub | Sub 1(stop) |
| Switch off the green light 3 and switch on the warning yellow light 2 for vehicles. | Turn off Output 3. Turn on Output 2. | Input Output |
| Allow the light to stay on for 2 seconds. | Delay 2 | Process |
| Switch off the yellow light 2 and the red stop light 4; switch on the green light 5 (for the pedestrian crossing) and the red light 1 (to stop the vehicles). | Turn off Outputs 2 and 4. Turn on Outputs 5 and 1. | Input Output |
| Allow the lights to stay on for 8 seconds. | Delay 8 | Process |
| Switch off the green light 5 and the red light 1. | Turn off Outputs 5 and 1. | Input Output |
| Stop the subroutine. | Stop | Stop |

## Subroutine 2

- We need another subroutine to flash the green light for the pedestrian as a warning that time is running out.
- The idea is just to switch the green light on and off.
- Use the table below to plan for the flashing subroutine to warn the pedestrian.
- Name the subroutine Sub 2(flash).

| Description of the event in ordinary words | Control words | Flowchart symbol |
|---|---|---|
| Begin the subroutine. | Sub | Sub 2 (stop) |
| Switch on the green light 5 to allow the pedestrian to cross and the red light 1 to stop vehicles. | Turn on Output 1 and Output 5 | Input Output |
| Allow the lights to stay on for 5 seconds. | Delay 5 | Process |
| Switch off the green light 5. | Turn off Output 5 | Input Output |
| Allow a time lapse of 5 seconds. | Delay 5 | Process |
| Stop the subroutine. | Stop | Stop |

- To flash the light, repeat this subroutine a few times.

## The main routine

- You will need a main routine to command the subroutines.
- Use the table below to plan for the main routine.
- Name the main routine as main.

| Description of the event in ordinary words | Control words | Flowchart symbol |
|---|---|---|
| Begin the main routine. | Start | Start |
| Switch on the red light 4 to stop the pedestrian crossing and the green light 3 to allow vehicles to continue. | Turn on Output 1 and Output 4 | Input Output |
| Decision: is Input 1 on? | Decision | |
| If Input 1 is not on, loop back. | Loop | |
| If Input 1 is on, activate Sub 1(stop). | Sub | |
| Activate Sub 2(flash) five times to flash the light. | Sub x 5 | |
| Switch off the red light. | Turn off Output 1 | Input Output |
| Loop back to check the input. | Loop | |

## Testing and evaluation

- Test-run the system with simulation software. You may need to change the name of the output or input to suit the simulation test.

- Compare the system with a real-life system and discuss what possible changes you should make to improve the system.

    Hints:   1.   Compare the time delay of the system with the real-life system. Is the time delay long enough in terms of safety?

    2.   What are the limitations of the system?

    3.   What possible problems could be encountered with the system?

    4.   What further safety precautions could be taken?

    5.   Make sensible suggestions to improve the system.

    ....................................................................................................

    ....................................................................................................

    ....................................................................................................

    ....................................................................................................

    ....................................................................................................

    ....................................................................................................

    ....................................................................................................

    ....................................................................................................

    ....................................................................................................

    ....................................................................................................

    ....................................................................................................

- Save your flowchart as traffic4.

- Re-test your flowchart using the software and make any further changes needed. List any changes that you make in the space below.

    ....................................................................................................

    ....................................................................................................

    ....................................................................................................

    ....................................................................................................

    ....................................................................................................

## Level-crossing barrier

- When the train is crossing, the barrier is lowered to close the road to prevent vehicles from crossing.
- When the train has passed, the barrier is lifted up to allow vehicles to cross again.
- The system is similar to a traffic-light system. However, a barrier, controlled by a motor, is used as an additional safeguard.

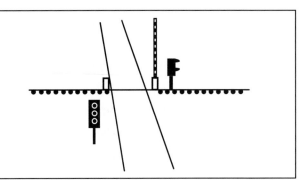

## The subroutine

- The following are the input and output devices.

| Input | Description |
|---|---|
| Input 1 | Device detecting approaching train |
| Input 2 | Device detecting train that has crossed |

| Output | Description |
|---|---|
| Output 1 | The motor controlling the level |
| Output 2 | Red light stopping train from crossing |
| Output 3 | Green light allowing train to cross |
| Output 4 | Red light stopping vehicles from crossing |
| Output 5 | Green light allowing vehicles to cross |

- First create the subroutines to control the barrier motor.

| Description of the event in ordinary words | Control words | Flowchart symbol |
|---|---|---|
| Begin the subroutine. | Sub | Sub 1(close) |
| Turn the motor on. | Turn motor forward | |
| Allow 5 seconds' time lapse. | Delay 5 | |
| Turn the motor off. | Turn motor off | |
| Stop the subroutine. | Stop | Stop |

| Description of the event in ordinary words | Control words | Flowchart symbol |
|---|---|---|
| Begin the subroutine. | Sub | |
| Turn the motor on (reverse). | Turn motor reverse | |
| Allow 5 seconds' time lapse. | Delay 5 | |
| Turn the motor off. | Turn motor off | |
| Stop the subroutine. | Stop | |

## The main routine

- Now construct the main routine to command the subroutines.
- Test the system with simulation software.
- You may have to adjust the input and output labels to suit the software.
- Save your work as lvcross1.
- Create subroutines to control the traffic flow on the road.
- You can flash the green light (Output 5) to give warning.
- Save your new work as lvcross2.

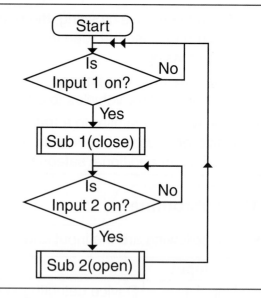

## Evaluation

- Compare the system with a real-life situation.
- Can the system really work?
- Is it really safe?
- Consider what will happen if there is a power failure.
- What will happen if the motor is malfunctioning?
- Will all the drivers or road users follow the signals as they should?
- What will happen if they don't?
- With the modern technology used in building roads, is there a better substitute for the system?
- Would a flyover work better?

## Analogue sensors

- Temperature and brightness are two important variable inputs for controlling certain utilities in a house.
- For example, when the temperature drops below a pre-set level, the electric fire is set to switch on automatically. It is set to switch off automatically when the temperature rises above the pre-set level again.
- Different simulation software packages use different pictures to symbolise the temperature control.
- Some temperature controls can be stepped up or down by 5 or 10 degrees.
- Try a similar flowchart on your software and save your work as fire1.

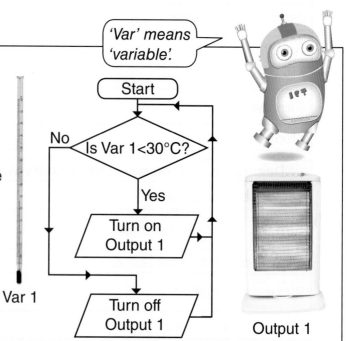

'Var' means 'variable'.

# Ventilation control

- Temperature varies and affects the use of ventilation.
- Create a similar flowchart to control the ventilation fan, using the temperature as variable inputs.
- Save your work as fan1.

| Input | Description |
|-------|-------------|
| Var 1 | Temperature control |

| Output | Description |
|--------|-------------|
| Output 2 | Ventilation fan |

- Certain software packages allow two or more main systems to run at the same time.
- Since the electric heater and the ventilation fan both use the variable temperature as input, using the same variable input name allows the two systems to be tested simultaneously.

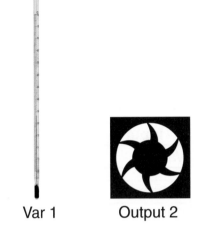

Var 1          Output 2

# Brightness input

- Brightness is always a factor when considering whether to open the blinds at the windows or switch on the lights in the room.
- This system is similar to the system for controlling the ventilation fan and electric heater.
- Use the following list of input and outputs to create the system and save it as brightness.

| Input | Description |
|-------|-------------|
| Var 2 | Brightness control (sun) |

| Output | Description |
|--------|-------------|
| Output 3 | Lamp |
| Output 4 | Electric blinds |

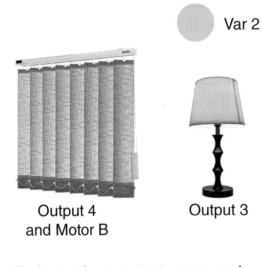

Var 2

Output 4          Output 3
and Motor B

- While the lamp is a simple on-and-off system, the electric blinds require a motor to open and close (reverse) them.
- Construct two subroutines, one to turn on the motor and the other one to close (reverse) the motor.
- Construct another main routine to command the 2 subroutines.
- Test the systems and compare them with real-life situations.
- What are the limitations of the systems?

  ....................................................................................................................

  ....................................................................................................................

- What are the possible problems that may affect the systems in real life?

  ....................................................................................................................

### The greenhouse

- A greenhouse allows you to grow fresh vegetables, flowers and herbs all year round. The temperature, brightness and humidity need to be controlled properly.

- Certain herbs cultivated in a greenhouse require the temperature to be kept above 30°C and below 50°C. A heat sensor, a heater and a ventilation window control the temperature in the greenhouse.

- Here is a list of the input and outputs that are used:

| Input | Description |
|---|---|
| Var 1 | Heat sensor (thermometer) |

| Output | Description |
|---|---|
| Output 1 | Heater |
| Output 2 | Ventilation window |

### Temperature-control system

- Use the table below to plan a simple temperature-control system for the greenhouse.

| Description of the event in ordinary words | Control words | Flowchart symbol |
|---|---|---|
| Begin the system. | Start | ( Start ) |
| Check the lowest temperature limit. | Is Var<30°C? | < Decision > |
| If the temperature <30°C, turn on the heater. | Yes | / Output / |
| If the temperature >30°C, turn off the heater. | No | / Output / |
| Repeat the checking of lowest temperature limit. | Loop | ⟶ |

| Description of the event in ordinary words | Control words | Flowchart symbol |
|---|---|---|
| Begin the system. | Start | ( Start ) |
| Check the upper temperature limit. | Is Var>50°C? | |
| | Yes | |
| | | |
| | | |

- Construct the flowcharts for the system using appropriate software.
- Save your flowcharts as greenhouse1.

## Testing

- Test your flowchart using the simulation software.

- As you increase or decrease the temperature, describe what happens:

  (i) when the temperature is below 30°C ..............................................................................

  .......................................................................................................................................

  (ii) when the temperature reaches 30°C ...............................................................................

  .......................................................................................................................................

  (iii) when the temperature reaches 50°C ..............................................................................

  .......................................................................................................................................

  (iv) when the temperature is above 50°C ..............................................................................

  .......................................................................................................................................

- Write down any problems or weaknesses of the system that you are testing.

  .......................................................................................................................................

  .......................................................................................................................................

  .......................................................................................................................................

  .......................................................................................................................................

  .......................................................................................................................................

- Make changes to resolve the problems that you have encountered above.

- Save your new flowchart as greenhouse2.

- Compare the system that you have designed with a real system. What are the limitations and possible problems that you may encounter?

  .......................................................................................................................................

  .......................................................................................................................................

  .......................................................................................................................................

  .......................................................................................................................................

  .......................................................................................................................................

  .......................................................................................................................................

## Variables

- We can use a letter to represent a value that is not fixed and that keeps changing.
- We call the letter a variable.
- A variable can be added or subtracted.
- For example:

  Let $n = 1$

  Let $n = n + 1$

  Let $n = n - 1$

- We can use the variable to create a counter to count the number of cars entering or leaving a car park.
- In this way, we can inform car drivers when the car park is full.
- A car-park controlling system adds the number of cars to the counter as it allows them to enter; it subtracts the number of cars from the counter as it allows them to leave. When the number of cars entering the car park has reached its maximum capacity, a 'Car Park Full' sign is lit and no more cars are allowed to enter.
- Here is a list of the input and output devices that are used:

| Input | Description |
|---|---|
| Input 1 | Detects an incoming car |
| Input 2 | Detects the incoming car passing the barrier |
| Input 3 | Detects an outgoing car |
| Input 4 | Detects the outgoing car passing the barrier |

| Output | Description |
|---|---|
| Output 1 | Barrier controls incoming cars |
| Output 2 | Barrier controls outgoing cars |
| Output 3 | 'Car Park Full' sign |

- Complete the table below and use it to plan one subroutine to control incoming cars.

| Description of the event in ordinary words | Control words | Flowchart symbol |
|---|---|---|
| Begin the system. | Start | |
| Open the barrier. | Turn on Output 1 (Motor a) | |
| Delay for 2 seconds. | Delay 2 | |
| Turn off the motor. | Turn off Output 1 (Motor a) | |
| End the system. | Stop | |

- Design a similar subroutine for opening the barrier for an outgoing car.

# Counter

- Complete the table below and use it to plan one subroutine to close the barrier after an incoming car and to add 1 to the counter.

| Description of the event in ordinary words | Control words | Flowchart symbol |
|---|---|---|
| Begin the system. | Start | |
| Close the barrier. | Reverse Output 1 (Motor a) | |
| Delay for 2 seconds. | Delay 2 | |
| Turn off the motor. | Turn off Output 1 (Motor a) | |
| Add 1 to the counter. | Let n = n+1 | |
| End the system. | Stop | |

- Design a similar subroutine for closing the barrier for an outgoing car and to subtract 1 from the counter.

# 'Car Park Full' sign

- Complete the table below and use it to plan one main routine to check the number of incoming cars and to light the 'Car Park Full' sign when the number of incoming cars reaches 4.
  (For testing purposes, the number suggested is small.)

| Description of the event in ordinary words | Control words | Flowchart symbol |
|---|---|---|
| Begin the system. | Start | |
| Is the counter greater than 4? | Is n > 4? | |
| If the counter is greater than 4, light the 'Car Park Full' sign. | Turn on Output 3 | |
| If the counter is less than 4, turn off the 'Car Park Full' sign. | Turn off Output 3 | |
| End the system. | Stop | |

- Save your work as barrier1.

## Car park main routine

- Complete the following table and use it to plan for the main routine to command the 2 subroutines that control the barrier for incoming cars.

| Description of the event in ordinary words | Control words | Flowchart symbol |
|---|---|---|
| Begin the system. | | |
| Is there a car coming in? | Is Input 1 on? | |
| Yes: command the subroutine to open the barrier. | | |
| No: loop back to wait for input. | | |
| Has the car passed the barrier? | Is Input 2 on? | |
| Yes: command the subroutine to close the barrier. | | |
| No: loop to wait for the car to pass. | | |

- Design a similar main routine to command the other two subroutines to control the outgoing cars.
- Save your flowcharts as barrier2.

## Testing and evaluation

- Test the whole system using the simulation software.

- In the simulation software that you are using to test the system, how do you simulate the incoming car?

   ..............................................................................................................................

- Is there a counter to show the number of cars going in and out? If not, how would you know that when the 'Car Park Full' sign is lit, the number of cars counted by the counter is the actual maximum limit specified?

   ..............................................................................................................................

   ..............................................................................................................................

   ..............................................................................................................................

   ..............................................................................................................................

   ..............................................................................................................................

## Identify limitations

- In the design, the barrier is still open when the 'Car Park Full' sign is lit. Improve the system so that when the car park is full, the barrier will not open even if Input 1 is on.

- Add a sound effect to alert the incoming cars that the car park is full when the Input 1 detects there is an incoming car.

- Save your improved flowchart as barrier3.

- Compare the system with a real-life situation. What are the limitations of the system that you have just designed?

  You can also write about the problems that may be faced in real life. For example, when there is:

  ○ a power failure (the system has no manual mechanism)

  ○ a mechanical breakdown or malfunction of a barrier

  ○ a human error, etc.

..............................................................................................................................

..............................................................................................................................

..............................................................................................................................

..............................................................................................................................

..............................................................................................................................

..............................................................................................................................

..............................................................................................................................

..............................................................................................................................

..............................................................................................................................

..............................................................................................................................

..............................................................................................................................

..............................................................................................................................

..............................................................................................................................

..............................................................................................................................

..............................................................................................................................

..............................................................................................................................

..............................................................................................................................

..............................................................................................................................

# Optional extension and challenge activities

## Module 5 – Control for a Purpose

### Challenge 1

You have been asked to design a security system on paper to protect a valuable diamond. Explain ways in which you can protect it using detectors and alarms. Detectors might include devices to check that the diamond is on its stand. Beams of light might be broken by a burglar approaching the diamond.

### Challenge 2

- Build a sequence of events to activate a warning system for a lighthouse if the weather is foggy. The light should flash 3 times, delay two seconds, with a fog-horn sounding twice, followed by a delay of 4 seconds before one flash.

- Decide on your own time between each complete sequence.

- Use flowchart symbols to record your idea.

# Optional extension and challenge activities

**Challenge 3**

Evaluate a system you have designed. Work with a friend to suggest ways to improve or develop it further.

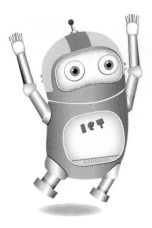

# Module 6
# Website Design for a Purpose

## Learning Objectives

| | Student is able to: | Pass/Merit |
|---|---|---|
| 1 | Create a series of connected web pages | P |
| 2 | Include links | P |
| 3 | Insert images | P |
| 4 | Demonstrate user awareness | M |
| 5 | Recognise HTML code | M |

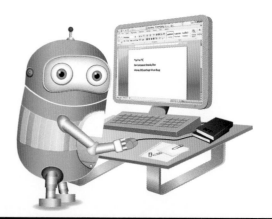

# 6.1 Designing a website

## What is HTML?

- HTML stands for Hypertext Markup Language.
- An HTML file is a text file containing small markup tags.
- The markup tags tell the Web browser how to display the page.
- An HTML file must have an htm or html file extension.
- An HTML file can be created using a simple text editor like Notepad on Windows.
- You can easily edit HTML files using a Web page editor such as Microsoft Expression Web 4, instead of writing your markup tags in a plain-text file.

*For beginners, it would be a lot easier to design your first website with the aid of a web page editor.*

*So for our exercises, we will be using Microsoft Expression Web 4 to start our first web project.*

## Good website design

- To become a good website designer, you will have to be aware of the needs of your audiences:
  - Font type, size and colour should be readable and should not strain your audience's eyes
  - Hyperlinks, hotspots and navigation menu should be working and valid
  - Images should not take too long to download, so always check the size of the image file you are planning to use
  - Consistent layout design and style in all your web pages.
- List down what you like and don't like about the design of any website you have visited recently:

  ..................................................................

  ..................................................................

  ..................................................................

  ..................................................................

  ..................................................................

  ..................................................................

  ..................................................................

  ..................................................................

  ..................................................................

  ..................................................................

  ..................................................................

*Print out that web page and glue it here!*

## Opening Microsoft Expression

- To run Microsoft Expression Web 4, do the following:
  - On the Windows taskbar,

    click, point to ▶ All Programs.

    and then click Microsoft Expression.

    and then click Microsoft Expression Web 4.
  - If this is the first time you've used Microsoft Expression, the program opens and displays a blank page ready for editing.

*If Microsoft Expression has been used to edit another website, it will open the last website automatically.*

*To close a website:* go to File and click Close.

## Workspace overview

- The following table and graphic highlight some of the commonly used features in Microsoft Expression Web 4.

| Menus and toolbars | These allow you to perform tasks such as saving files and sites, generating reports, and changing how you view a page. |
| --- | --- |
| Panels | These allow you to perform tasks such as managing files in a site, adding tags to a page, and managing styles. |
| Editing window | It allows you to visually edit pages or directly edit page markup. |
| Status Bar | It shows you important information about sites and pages. |

## The editing window

- When your site is open, the Site View tab is displayed at the top of the editing window.

- The files you have opened appear as tabs at the top of the editing window.

- Click on a tab to edit a page.

- The file you are currently editing is highlighted.

- Pages can be edited in Design, Split or Code view. For most of the following tasks you will use Design view.

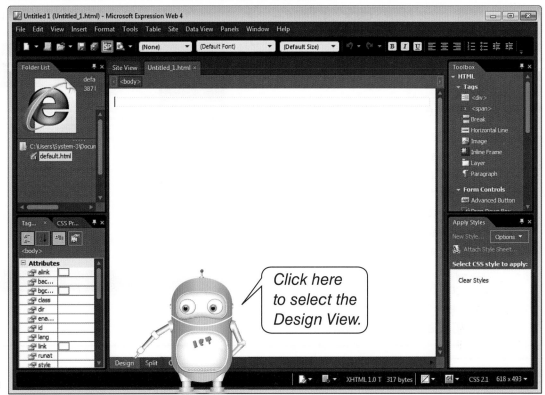

*Click here to select the Design View.*

## Creating a new site

- On the toolbar, click ▤ to open a new site.

- In the middle column, click ▤ Empty Site to create a folder (where you will store the files for your website).

- Click Browse... to find the folder where you want to save your site.

- Click Open and the Location box will now show where the site will be saved.

- In the Location box, type BORNEO after the folder name. You will see the website name appear in the Name box as you do this.

- Click OK. All the files and folders for your website will be stored in this folder.

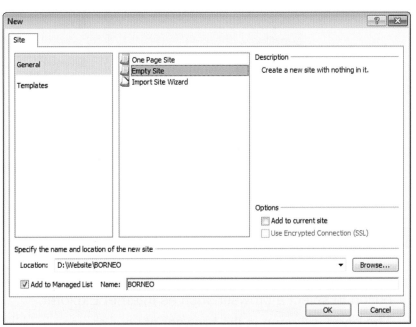

## Creating a homepage

- Click **File**, click **New**, click **Page...**, select **HTML** and then click **OK**.

- Type BORNEO on the Home page and then tap **⏎ Enter** twice.

- Next, type the paragraph below:

  Borneo is a large island in South East Asia that comprises the sultanate of Brunei, Indonesia and Malaysia. The tiny nation of Brunei is wedged between two Malaysian states. The Indonesian part of Borneo consists of the southern two-thirds of the island's area and is divided into the four provinces of West, Central, South and East Kalimantan. The Malaysian part comprises the northern coast and is divided into the states of Sabah and Sarawak.

- Your page should now look like this:

## Saving the current page

- Click **File** and **Save**.

- In the File name box, type Home Page and click **Save**.

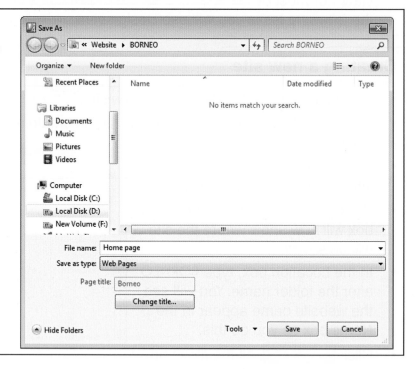

## Previewing the page

- To see how your page will look on the Web, click preview or click the arrow next to the button to select a browser such as Internet Explorer.

- The page will open in the browser of your choice.

## Adding a new page

- Click [☰ ▼], click [] Page..., select [⊙] HTML and then click [ OK ].
- On the blank page in Design view, type GEOGRAPHY and then tap [←Enter] twice.
- Next, type the paragraph below:

  Borneo is the third largest island in the world, surrounded by the South China Sea to the north and north-west, the Sulu Sea to the north-east, the Celebes Sea and the Makassar Strait to the east, and the Java Sea and Karimata Strait to the south. It has an area of 743,330 km$^2$ (287,000 square miles), and is located at the centre of the Malay Archipelago and Indonesia. Borneo is considered to be part of the geographic region of South East Asia.

- Save this page as:
  - Page title – Geography
  - File name – Geography
- You will now see your files and folder in the Folder List.

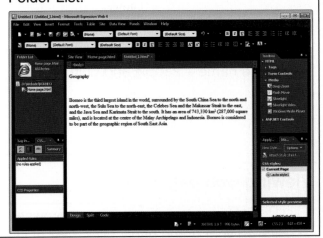

## Adding another page

- Open the Word document file Government and Administration.
- Select all the content and click [📋] Copy.
- Go back to Microsoft Expression Web 4 and click [☰ ▼].
- Then click [Edit].
- Then click [📋 Paste                    Ctrl+V].
- Save this page as:
  - Page title – Government and Administration
  - File name – Government and Administration
- Your page should now look like this:

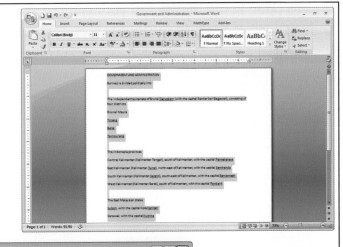

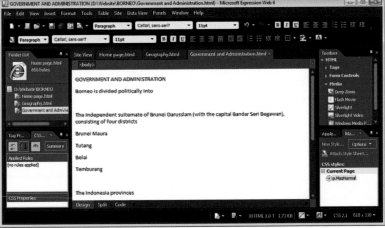

## Adding the final page

- Open the Word document file People and Culture.

- Select and copy all the content in the document, then paste on to a new page in Microsoft Expression Web 4.

- Save this page as:
  - Page title – People and Culture
  - File name – People and Culture.

- Your page should now look like this:

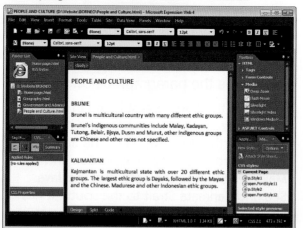

## Viewing web pages

- To see how your pages look in a browser, click on your home page, click [button] or click the arrow next to the button to select a browser such as Internet Explorer. The page will open in the browser of your choice.

- View all the other web pages you have created.

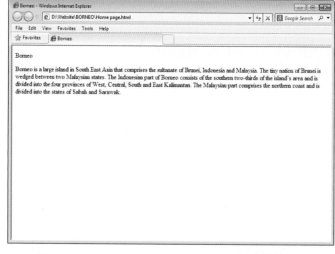

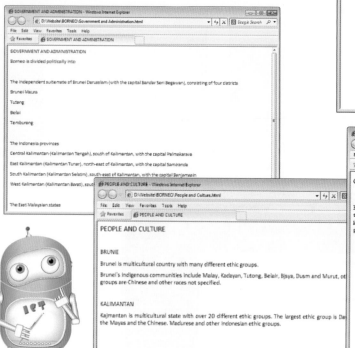

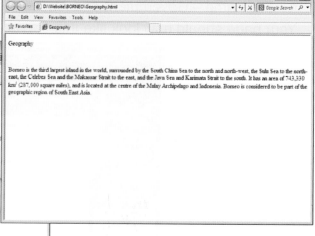

# 6.4 Creating hyperlinks

## Adding links

- Go back to your previous work Borneo.
- At the end of the last paragraph, tap  twice.
- Type:

  GEOGRAPHY

  GOVERNMENT AND ADMINISTRATION

  PEOPLE AND CULTURE.
- Save your work.

## Linking web pages

- Select the text GEOGRAPHY.
- Click 🖥 on the Standard toolbar.
- In the Insert Hyperlink dialog box, click **Existing File or Web Page**.
- Browse through your folder, select your web page Geography and click ⎡ OK ⎤.
- Save your work.
- Select the Home page in Site view, and click 🖳▼.
- Click on the coloured and underlined text <u>GEOGRAPHY</u>.
- It should bring you to the page you created previously, titled Geography.

## Internal links

- Return to the Home page.
- Select the text GOVERNMENT AND ADMINISTRATION.
- Click 🖥.
- Click **Existing File or Web Page**.

- Browse through your folder, select your web page Government and Administration and click ⎡ OK ⎤.
- Repeat the previous steps for the text PEOPLE AND CULTURE and link it to the page People and Culture.
- Save your work.

## Linking to other websites

- Go back to your previous work Borneo.

- At the end of the last text People and Culture, tap twice.

- Type this sentence:

  If you would like to know more about Borneo, go to VisitBorneo.com.

- Select the text VisitBorneo.com.

- Click .

- In the Insert Hyperlink dialog box, type the following web address in

  Address: |       ▼ www.visitborneo.com.

- Click OK.

- Save your work.

- Now preview the page by clicking at the bottom of the page.

- Click on the coloured and underlined text VisitBorneo.com.

  It should bring you to the page titled VisitBorneo.com as shown below:

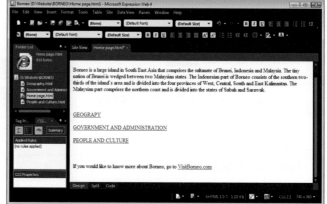

## External links

- Go back to your previous work Borneo.

- In the paragraph, select the word Brunei in the second sentence after the text 'The tiny nation of'.

- Click .

- Type the following web address in

  Address: |       ▼ www.tourismbrunei.com.

- Click OK.

- Repeat the steps again for:

| Word | Link to |
|------|---------|
| Kalimantan | www.e-borneo.com/ infoborneo/kal-tourism. shtml |
| Sabah | www.sabahtourism.com |
| Sarawak | www.sarawaktourism.com |

- Save you work.

### Inserting an image

- Go back to your previous work Borneo in the Design view.

- At the end of the title BORNEO, tap ⟵Enter once.
- Click **Insert**, select **Picture** and then click 🖼 **From File...** .
- In the Picture dialog box, use the drop-down box to browse through your folder for the image file Borneo map.
- Select the file, click **Insert**, and then click ⬜ OK without adding anything to the next dialog box.

*A short cut to insert an image is made available by clicking 🖼 on the Toolbar.*

### Resizing an image

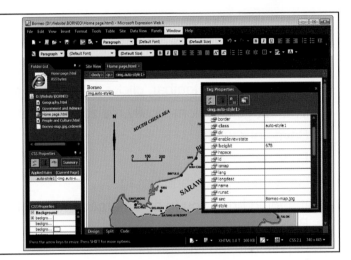

- Select the Borneo map image.
- On **Format**, select **Tag Properties...** .
- Look in the **Tag Properties...** panel.
- In Width: [650] ⬍, change the number specified to 350.
- In Height: [678] ⬍, change the number specified to 365.
- Click ⬜ OK .
- Your inserted image should now fit comfortably in your web page.

### Aligning the image

- Select the Borneo map image again.
- On the Formatting toolbar, click ▤.
- The image should automatically align to the left.
- Click ▤, and the image is now right-aligned.
- Click ▤ again.
- Now click ▤, and the image is centred.
- Save your work.
- If the image does not centre this way, double-click on it to bring up the Picture Properties dialogue box. Click the Appearance tab and click  in

  None

  the Wrapping style option. You may then use the align icons or drag to centre the image.
- Preview the page.

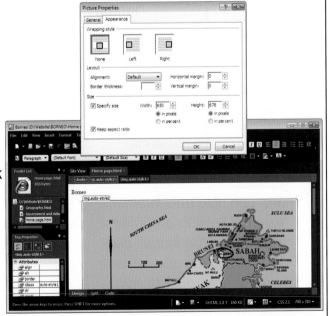

## Auto thumbnail

- Go back to your previous work Geography in the Design view.

- At the end of the paragraph, tap ⏎Enter twice.

- Type:

  Map of Borneo

  Map of Brunei

  Map of Kalimantan

  Map of Sabah

  Map of Sarawak.

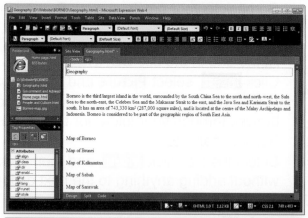

- At the end of the title, Map of Borneo, tap ⏎Enter once.

- Insert the image Borneo map.

- Select the image.

- On the Pictures toolbar, click 🖼 Auto Thumbnail.

- The image is automatically resized into a thumbnail.

- Save your work.

- Preview the page.

- Click on the thumbnail image.

- It should bring you to an enlarged image of the Borneo map.

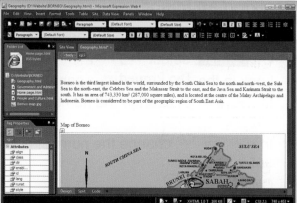

- Go back to the Design view.

  Repeat the steps above to create thumbnails for the rest in the list:

| Map | Image |
|-----|-------|
| Brunei | Brunei map |
| Kalimantan | Kalimantan map |
| Sabah | Sabah map |
| Sarawak | Sarawak map |

- Save your work.

*You can also add internal or external links to any image. Just select the image, click 🌐, then follow the steps to add the appropriate link.*

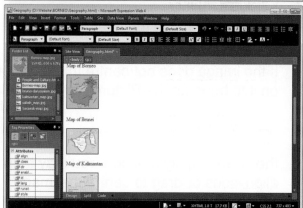

# 6.6 Navigation menu

## Navigation options

- Go back to your previous work Borneo in the Design view.
- At the end of the sentence 'If you would...', tap [←Enter] twice.
- In **Insert**, point to HTML ▶, Click ▬ Horizontal Line.
- Tap [←Enter] again.
- Type: NEXT SECTION >.
- Select the text NEXT SECTION >.
- Click ≡: this centres the text.
- Then click 🔗 to link this text to the Geography page.
- Click [ OK ].
- Save your work.

- Now preview the page.
- Click on the coloured and underlined text NEXT SECTION >.
- It should bring you to the page entitled Geography.

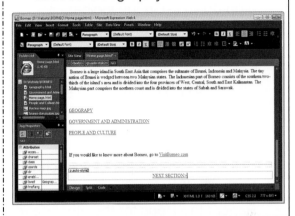

## Consistent navigation

- Go back to your previous work Geography in the Design view.
- At the end of the page, tap [←Enter] twice.
- In **Insert**, point to HTML ▶, Click ▬ Horizontal Line.
- Tap [←Enter] again.
- Type: < GO BACK TO HOME.
- Then tap [←Tab] once.
- Now type: NEXT SECTION >.
- Select both text < GO BACK TO HOME and NEXT SECTION >.
- Click ≡: this centres the selected text. Now repeat the steps to link each text to the appropriate page:

| Text | Link to page |
|------|-------------|
| <GO BACK TO HOME | Borneo |
| NEXT SECTION> | Government and Administration |

- Save your work.
- Add these navigation options to your other works Government and Administration and People and Culture.
- Refer to the tables on the right.

- For the page Government and Administration:

| Text | Link to page |
|------|-------------|
| <GO BACK TO HOME | Borneo |
| NEXT SECTION> | Government and Administration |

- For the page People and Culture:

| Text | Link to page |
|------|-------------|
| <GO BACK TO HOME | Borneo |

*Remember to centre all the text, so that every page has the same layout style.*

*It's a very good practice to save your work after completing each task.*

*Remember to save all the images used on your web pages within the same folder of your web project.*

## Headings

- Go back to your previous work Government and Administration in the Design view.
- Select the heading GOVERNMENT AND ADMINISTRATION.
- Select | Arial, Helvetica, sans-seri ▼ | from the fonts drop-down list in the toolbar.
- Select | x-large ▼ | from the | (Default Size) ▼ | list.
- Then click [B] to embolden the heading.
- Now click ▤.
- Click ▼ next to [A] ▼.
- Select the font colour of your choice. Click [ Apply ].
- Repeat the steps for the other headings in your other pages.

## Body text

- In the same page, select the text (with the capital Bandar Seri Begawan).
- Now click [I] to italicise the text.
- This will add some emphasis to the bracketed text.
- Repeat the steps for the other words in brackets on this page.
- Save your work.

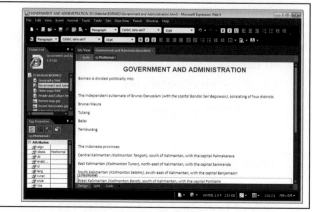

## Subheadings

- Go back to your previous work People and Culture in the Design view.
- Select the subheading BRUNEI.
- Then click [U] to underline the text.
- This will distinguish the subheading from the body text.
- Repeat the steps for the other subheadings on this page.
- Save your work.

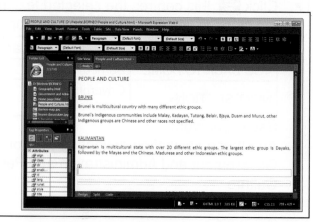

# 6.8 HTML code

## HTML coding

- Go back to your previous work Borneo in the HTML view.
- Print this page.
- In the Design view, select the heading BORNEO.
- Return to the HTML view and list the HTML tags used to code this heading:

| HTML tag | Used to code: |
|----------|---------------|
|          |               |
|          |               |
|          |               |
|          |               |
|          |               |

- Each HTML tag starts with a <?> and closes with the corresponding </?>.
- Highlight other tags used to code hyperlinks and images on your printout.

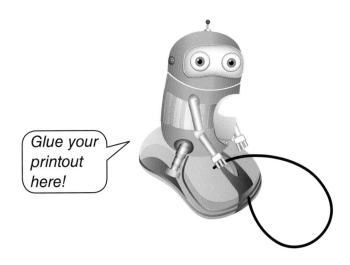

Glue your printout here!

# Optional extension and challenge activities

## Module 6 – Website Design for a Purpose

### Challenge 1

- Create a set of connected web pages using hyperlinks, to present a class magazine on the activities and achievements of your class.

### Challenge 2

Create a web-mag for your friends.
- You might include spot the difference pictures, anagrams, poems, puzzles and jokes.
- Put the answers on webpages at the end of the web-mag.
- Have a home page which includes the title of the web-mag and its contents.

### Challenge 3

- Add some recipe pages for your web-mag.
- Search the Internet to find recipes suitable for children to make.
- Copy some images to add to text which you write yourself.

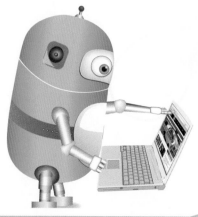

# Module 7
# Networks for a Purpose

## Learning Objectives

| | Student is able to: | Pass/Merit |
|---|---|---|
| 1 | Design a simple network | P |
| 2 | Identify the purpose and components of a network | P |
| 3 | Demonstrate understanding of management issues associated with networks | M |
| 4 | Understand network security issues | M |

## What is a network?

- Networks come in all shapes and sizes.
- They have many different uses.
- Landline telephones are connected to the telephone network.
- Mobile phones are connected to a wireless network.
- Computer networks allow computers to communicate with other computers. You can use them to share scanners and printers.
- Email is a form of communication using a computer network.
- Instant messaging is another example of using a computer network.

## What are the benefits?

*There are lots of advantages of using a network.*

- You can share scanners and printers with other people.

*Ten people can all share one printer.*

- You can share files with other people.

*Users on the same network can work on the same projects at the same time.*

- You can communicate with other people on your computer.

*Email means that you can send messages to, and receive them from, other people.*

- One person or computer can back up everyone's files.

*You can keep information safe by archiving it automatically.*

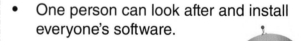

- One person can look after and install everyone's software.

*You can upgrade lots of people's software from one computer.*

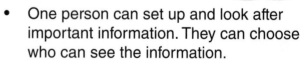

- One person can set up and look after important information. They can choose who can see the information.

*The people who need the important information can see it. People who don't need it can't.*

# What makes a network?

*A network is made of nodes, transmission media and hardware.*

## Nodes

- A node is a device on the network, e.g. a printer, scanner or workstation computer. It is a device that people interact with.

## Transmission media

- Transmission media are the ways in which the parts of the network are linked.
- Networks have a path to pass information along. This can be a cable or a wireless link that joins the two devices.

## Network hardware

- Network hardware includes the devices used to connect all the nodes on a network.
- It provides network services such as print servers and file servers.

# Types of network

*There are two main types of network.*

## Transmission media

- LANs or Local Area Networks are the networks that connect computers and network devices in a room or a building. They connect computers and network devices over short distances.
- WANs or Wide Area Networks are networks that cover a big area. They connect individual computers or LANs over big distances.

# Ask yourself

*What kinds of network are these? LAN or WAN?*

- Fifteen computers in an IT suite.

  ......................................................

- The school network to networks in other schools in your area.

  ......................................................

- Five IT suites in the same school each with their own network.

  ......................................................

- The school IT Manager's home PC to their PC in the school office using the telephone network.

  ......................................................

## Cables and wireless

- Just like telephone lines, computer networks use a variety of cables and ways to communicate.

- UTP (Unshielded Twisted Pair) cables are made from plastic-coated metal. Electricity can pass through them.

- Fibre optics are cables made from glass fibres. Light can pass through them.

- Wireless uses radio waves to pass on messages.

- Infrared devices use heat waves to communicate. Most TV control pads are infrared.

## Hubs

- A hub is a device that connects a network to several devices at once.

- Most hubs have 8, 16 or 32 sockets for the cable jacks to plug into.

- Hubs have a socket for connecting to other hubs or switches.

- A hub passes information it receives from one node to all the other connected nodes.

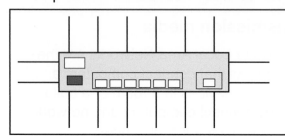

One hub can be connected to another hub to increase the number of nodes that can be joined together. In the most common networks, each cable has a maximum length of 100 metres. Hubs usually connect nodes in a small area, e.g. a single floor in an office block. They work best on networks where there is little network traffic.

## Switches

- A switch is a device that connects different sections of a network. Switches work in a similar way to hubs. They usually connect one hub to another hub.

- For example, they can connect the networks on each floor of a multi-storey office. Also, they make the network more efficient because they pass information only to the section of the network that needs it, rather than sending it to all the sections of the network.

- On busy networks with many hubs, the hubs are connected together using switches.

- A switch is a clever hub, really.

## Servers

- A server is a computer or device on a network that manages network resources.

- A file server is used to store critical data for retrieval. Any authorised user on the network can store and retrieve files on the server.

- A print server is a computer that controls one or more printers.

- A server acts as the communications gateway between many computers connected to it, responding to requests for information from client computers.

- A server is also used for managing network traffic.

# Routers

- Routers connect one network to another. For example, a router can connect the network of a company's office in one city to that in another city.

- The network of the company's head office in another city can have a router to connect it to the same network.

- This allows the two offices to communicate with each other.

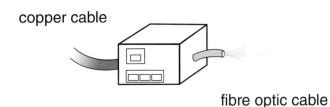

copper cable

fibre optic cable

- Routers can pass information from one transmission medium to a different one.

# Modems

- A modem is a device that converts digital signals from a computer to analogue signals that you can send over a standard telephone line and vice versa.

- It connects individual PCs using the telephone network.

# Bandwidth

- Bandwidth is a measure of how fast a network is.

- A high-bandwidth network can pass a lot of information in a short time.

- A low-bandwidth network passes a smaller amount of information in the same time.

# Network diagrams

- A network diagram is useful in displaying the set-up plan of the network.

- The diagram helps to identify the additional hardware needed.

- The diagram also helps to diagnose faults in the network.

- There is software specially designed for drawing network diagrams. However, the autoshapes set in Microsoft Word, Microsoft PowerPoint (or any word processing or presentation software), with a few additional pieces of clip art, are sufficient for drawing simple network diagrams.

- When drawing the links between peripherals, try to keep the lines neat; use vertical or horizontal lines.

- The diagram below shows a simple network connecting 4 computers and 1 printer, using a hub.

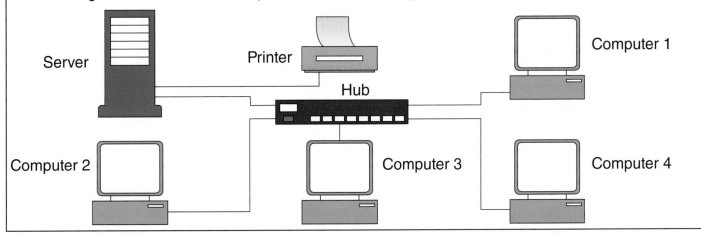

## Complex networks

- The diagram below shows a more complex network connecting 18 computers, 3 printers and 2 scanners through a router.

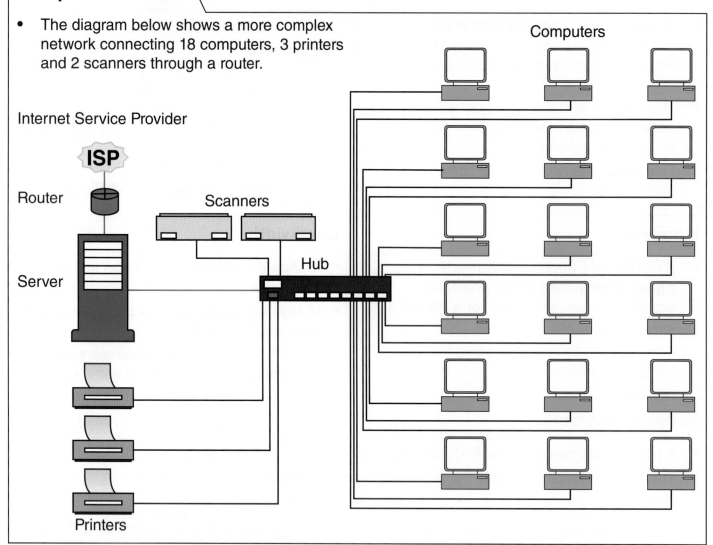

## Network management

- A network manager is usually appointed to ensure the smooth running of the network.
- The work of the network manager includes:
  - Configuration management
    - installing new hardware such as printers and drivers
    - installing new software
    - installing new firewall, antivirus and antispyware programs
    - registering new users
    - extending the network system to new computers
  - Fault finding
    - checking to see if all nodes are present
  - Security
    - setting up user accounts, changing passwords, setting permissions to use network resources
    - regularly backing up important data and keeping the backups in a safe location

### Advantages of using a network

- What are the advantages of connecting the many computers and the printers using a network?
  - All users can share the same printer, thus saving the cost of buying individual printers.
  - The money saved can be used to buy different types of printer.
  - Each user can choose between the different types of printer.
  - Users can save files to one location, the server, which all can access and from which backups can be made.
  - Users can share files and information directly from their computers, thus saving time and money.
  - Space is saved.
  - Once the network is connected to the Internet, all computers can access the Internet with only one Internet subscription.

### Disadvantages

- There are disadvantages of using a network too:
  - Lack of privacy: one user can view and access the information stored in the other computers in the network.
  - Lack of safety: one user may change or destroy the data or information in the other computers in the network without prior permission.
  - If the network goes down, the shared equipment, such as printers, will not function – and therefore everybody on the network will be affected.
  - There is more chance of virus attack and hacker attack.
  - If one computer is attacked by a virus, it can spread quickly to all the other computers in the same network.
  - It can slow down the Internet-access speed.
  - Improper use of shared equipment may affect the work of the other users.

### Management issues

- To enjoy the advantages and to reduce the disadvantages, steps must be taken to improve network efficiency. The following are some suggestions:
  - Users should be given some basic training before they are allowed to use the network. This will reduce the misuse of certain shared equipment.
  - Assign a network manager to look after the network. If there is a network breakdown and the manager is also the technician, the maintenance can be done immediately. If the manager is not the technician, the technician can be contacted to repair the network as soon as possible.
  - Use reliable licensed software and equipment.
  - Ensure that the essential components and drivers are easy to access.
  - Regularly check all connecting cables.
  - Regularly service the printers and other shared equipment.
  - Saving all files to a central server allows for easier backups.
  - Having a central file server allows network managers to update system software from one place.

# 7.3 Assignment 1

## Library network

- You are required to help design a simple network system for a school library with Internet connectivity, based on the following pieces of equipment and their respective locations.

| No. | Equipment | Location |
| --- | --- | --- |
| 1 | 1 computer, 1 scanner | Main entrance of the library |
| 2 | 1 computer, 1 printer | Head Librarian's room |
| 3 | 3 computers, 1 printer | General Office |

- What other hardware do you need to set up this network?

  .................................................................................................................................

  .................................................................................................................................

  .................................................................................................................................

  .................................................................................................................................

- Draw a network diagram to show how these need to be connected.

# Network components

- For each piece of hardware describe what it does on the network.

| Hardware | Function |
|---|---|
| Computer | Normally used by a single user for daily work such as word processing, keeping accounts, drawing and surfing the Internet. |
| Printer | Can be shared by users to print out hard copies of documents. |
| Scanner | |
| | |
| | |
| | |
| | |
| | |
| | |
| | |

- The network has been connected but the Head Librarian complains that the network is not stable; she is not able to access the Internet or the printers from the General Office. Suggest two changes to your network to ensure its efficiency and reliability.

    (1) Answer: ......................................................................................................................

         Reasons: ....................................................................................................................

         ....................................................................................................................................

    (2) Answer: ......................................................................................................................

         Reasons: ....................................................................................................................

         ....................................................................................................................................

## Safety and security

- In order to protect important data, here are some suggestions to help the network manager:
  - Install network-version virus-protection software in the network.
  - All users should be required to scan removable storage disks before they are used.
  - Use a log-in system. Every user is assigned an individual user name and password, and the entire log-in date and time should be recorded.
  - If necessary, use different passwords for access to different levels of the network system.
  - Set up a dial-up system for broadband Internet access. Only the manager and their assistants should be given the password to connect to the Internet.
  - Cultivate the habit of changing the password frequently.
  - Avoid using a shared-files folder; shared folders should be protected using passwords.
  - Computers should be in secure locations.
  - There should be regular backups of important data. The backup files must be kept in a safe place, preferably in a different building.
  - Only authorised persons are allowed to alter or install new software.
  - Consider using a firewall. This is a gateway to limit access between networks in the LAN to the WWW.

- Security measures vary from computer lab to computer lab. Write down any other suggestions that you think could improve the safety and security of the computer lab in which you work:

  .................................................................................................................................
  .................................................................................................................................
  .................................................................................................................................
  .................................................................................................................................
  .................................................................................................................................
  .................................................................................................................................

*Remember to change your password regularly.*

*Only authorised persons are allowed to access the network.*

# 7.4 Assignment 2

## Computer lab network

- You are required to help design a complete network system for a school computer lab with Internet connectivity, based on the following pieces of equipment and their respective locations.

| No. | Equipment | Location |
|-----|-----------|----------|
| 1 | 20 computers | Main Computer Lab |
| 2 | 1 computer, 1 printer, 1 scanner | Chief Supervisor's Office |
| 3 | 1 computer, 1 printer | Principal's Office |

- What other hardware do you need to set up this network?

..................................................................................................................................................

..................................................................................................................................................

..................................................................................................................................................

..................................................................................................................................................

- Draw a network diagram to show how these need to be connected.

# Hardware purpose

- For each piece of hardware describe what it does on the network.

| Hardware | Function |
|---|---|
| Computer | Normally used by a single user for daily work such as word processing, keeping accounts, drawing and surfing the Internet. |
| Printer | Can be shared by users to print out hard copies of documents. |
| | |
| | |
| | |
| | |
| | |
| | |
| | |

- The network has been connected but the Principal complains that the network is not stable; he is not able to access the Internet or any computer from the computer lab. Suggest two changes to your network to improve its efficiency and reliability.

(1) Answer: ...............................................................................................................

    Reasons: ..............................................................................................................

    .............................................................................................................................

(2) Answer: ...............................................................................................................

    Reasons: ..............................................................................................................

    .............................................................................................................................

# Safety

- In order to protect important data in the library system, suggest 5 actions that the network manager should take.

(1) Answer: ...................................................................................................................

Reasons: ...............................................................................................................

.................................................................................................................................

(2) Answer: ...................................................................................................................

Reasons: ...............................................................................................................

.................................................................................................................................

(3) Answer: ...................................................................................................................

Reasons: ...............................................................................................................

.................................................................................................................................

(4) Answer: ...................................................................................................................

Reasons: ...............................................................................................................

.................................................................................................................................

(5) Answer: ...................................................................................................................

Reasons: ...............................................................................................................

.................................................................................................................................

See page 48.

# Optional extension and challenge activities

## Module 7 – Networks for a Purpose

### Challenge 1

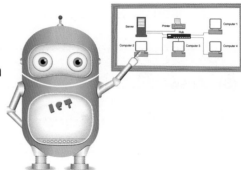

- On paper, design a simple network which shows how the computers for 4 classes are linked through a main hub.
- Show how the server is linked to the ISP.
- Add a scanner and printer for each pair of classes.

### Challenge 2

- Design a poster to persuade people of some of the advantages of using a network.

### Challenge 3

- Write an article for the school magazine which outlines problems to do with managing a network and dealing with some of the security issues.

# Module 8
# Video or Animation for a Purpose

## Learning Objectives

| | Student is able to: | Pass/Merit |
|---|---|---|
| 1 | Create a plan for video or animation | P |
| 2 | Create source material for video or animation | P |
| 3 | Produce video or animation with appropriate software | P |
| 4 | Add soundtrack or narration to video or animation | M |
| 5 | Demonstrate awareness of how the finished media text addresses a specific audience | M |

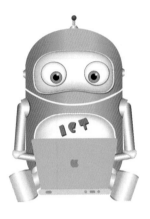

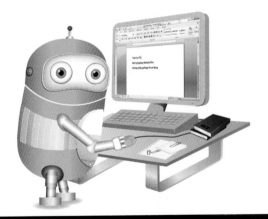

## Planning

- Animation is a series of graphics that simulate movement when viewed in sequence. The format of the graphics can depend on the software used.
- There is plenty of shareware and purchased-graphic software that can be used to produce animation.
- As with any other work, initial planning is very important.
- The initial planning or 'storyboard' can be drawn freehand.
- Use any graphics software to draw the graphics.
- The next section is a sample storyboard. Use this as an example to create your first animation project.

## Bullseye (storyboard)

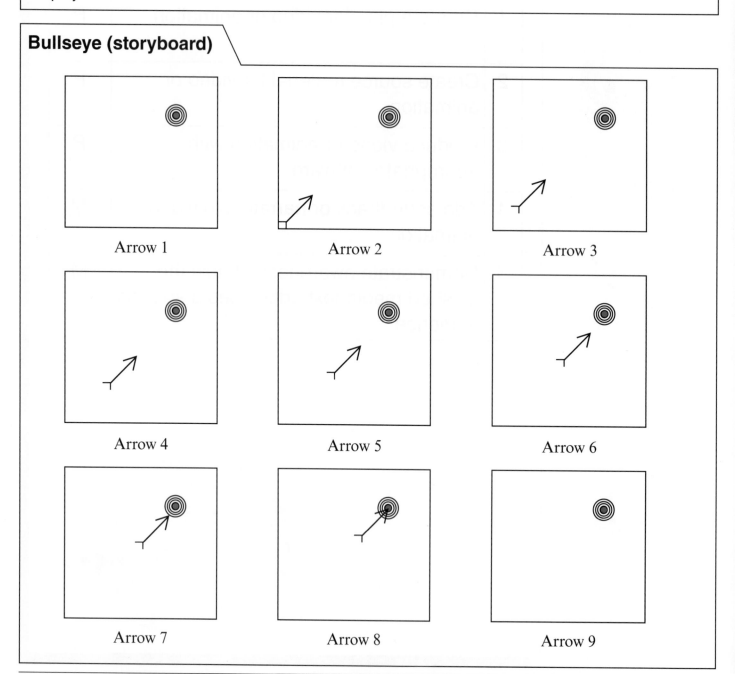

Arrow 1    Arrow 2    Arrow 3

Arrow 4    Arrow 5    Arrow 6

Arrow 7    Arrow 8    Arrow 9

# Preparing the graphics

- There are 9 pictures on the storyboard on the previous page.
- Use any graphics software (e.g. Paint) to create the pictures. Notice that pictures 1 and 9 are identical.
- When you begin drawing the pictures, draw the Arrow 1 picture first.
- Save it as arrow1.
- Save it again as arrow9.
- Add the arrow and save it as arrow2.
- Move the arrow further up and save it as arrow3.
- Similarly, by moving the arrow towards the bullseye, create the rest of the graphics: arrow4, arrow5 ... arrow9.
- Drawing the pictures this way will ensure that the bullseye remains at the exact position.
- This is important so that it will stay at the same position throughout the animation.
- Load Windows Movie Maker to create the animation.
- You can use other gif animators to create the animation too.

# Windows Movie Maker

- Load 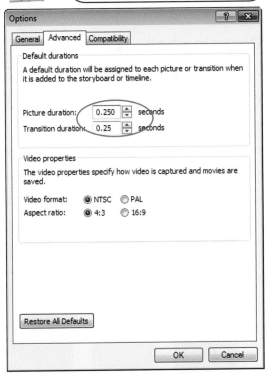 Windows Movie Maker 2.6 .
- Click File.
- Select Import into Collections... Ctrl+I .
- Go to the directory where you saved graphics and select all the pictures: arrow1, arrow2, ... arrow9.
- Click Import .
- Before you drag and drop the pictures into the storyboard, it is best to check the default setting of the duration.
- For the initial trial, set the picture duration and transition duration to 0.25 seconds.
- Click Tools and select Options... .
- Change the picture duration to 0.25 seconds.
- Change the transition duration to 0.25 seconds.
- Click OK .
- Drag and drop each of the pictures from arrow1 to arrow9 in the correct order into the storyboard.
- On the right-hand side is the preview window.
- Click (▶) to see the effect of the animation.
- Click File, select Save Project As... F12 and save the project as bullseye.mswmm.
- If the duration is not suitable, you can start again by first removing the pictures from the timeline.
- Click Edit and select Clear Timeline Ctrl+Del to remove the entire picture at the timeline.
- Try a few different durations until you find the one that you think is most appropriate.

*There are several versions of Windows Movie Maker. I have used Windows Movie Maker 2.6 here.*

## Making the movie

- When you have found the most appropriate duration for the animation, save the project again.

- To finalise the animation, you need to make it into a movie which can be viewed using the Microsoft Media Player.

- Click File, and select Save Movie File...  Ctrl+P .

- Select  My computer Save your movie for playback on your computer. as the location. Click Next > to continue.

- Type bullseye as the filename.

- Browse for your directory or folder to save the file and click Next > to continue.

- Accept the option and click Next > again to go to the next dialog page.

- Click Next > and the computer will start creating the movie.

- If you want to view the movie created immediately, click Finish ; otherwise uncheck the option before you click Finish .

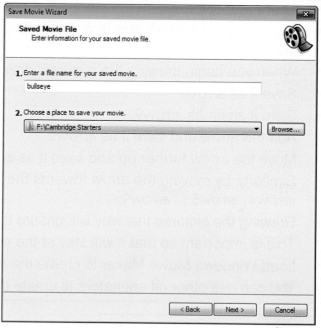

*The process of converting a series of images and sounds into a single movie file is called 'rendering'.*

## Dropping ball

- Use drawing software like Paint to draw the following pictures of balls.
- Save them as ball1, ball2, ball3, etc.
- Use these pictures to produce an animation of a ball dropping.
- Try different duration times and choose the most appropriate duration for your animation.
- Save the project as dropping_ball.
- Save the movie file as dropping_ball.

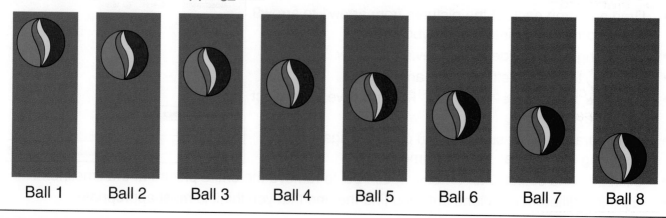

| Ball 1 | Ball 2 | Ball 3 | Ball 4 | Ball 5 | Ball 6 | Ball 7 | Ball 8 |

## Bouncing ball

- Open the project file dropping_ball.
- Rearrange the sequence of the pictures on the storyboard to ball2, ball4, ball6, ball8, ball7, ball5, ball3, ball4, ball6, ball8, ball6, ball4.
- Save the project file as bouncing.
- Preview the animation and adjust the duration so as to produce a bouncing ball.
- Save the movie file as bouncing.

## Changing the duration

- Instead of redoing the entire layout, you can change the duration for each individual picture.
- On the bottom panel, click ⊞ Show Timeline to display the timeline.

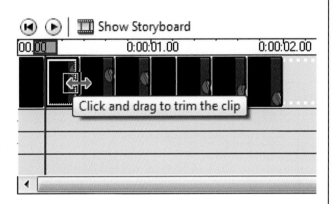

- Click 🔍 a few times to zoom in on the timeline.
- Click and drag at the edge to increase or decrease an individual frame of the picture.
- Instead of clicking ▶ to play the animation movie, you can just press and hold the space bar to play it.
- If you hold the space bar long enough, the animation will repeat itself until the space bar is released.

## More animation

- Choose one of the following topics or any topic of your own choice to create a new animation:
  - o  Football – penalty kick
  - o  Golf – the final stroke
  - o  Flying bird
- Use the space provided on the next page to plan the storyboard. You may use freehand drawing for the storyboard.
- Use a simple graphics software to create the graphics.
- You must create at least 5 different pictures.
- Write a brief description of what each frame is expected to show.
- Create the project file and save it as *your name* animation.
- Create the movie file and save it as *your name* animation1.

## Drafting

- Use this page for your draft storyboard. You may use freehand drawing for the draft.
- Give a brief description of each frame.

| | | |
|---|---|---|
| | | |
| | | |
| | | |

# Crossroads

- The following are the drafts of a new animation on crossroads.

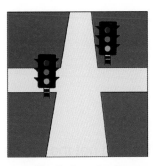

The traffic lights indicate green and the cars coming from the north–south direction may pass.

The approaching blue car continues its journey; the white car comes to a stop.

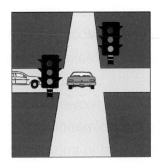

The blue car crosses the road.

The blue car continues past the crossroads.

The traffic lights change to yellow. The approaching red car prepares to stop; the white car prepares to cross in the east–west direction.

The red car stops and the white car crosses the road.

The white car has crossed the road and the traffic lights change to green again.

The red car crosses the road.

The red car continues past the crossroads.

## Creating the animation

- As in the previous section, before you create the animation you need to create the pictures.
- Think of your target audience and ensure that your creation meets its purpose. Improve your creation if necessary.
- You can draw or simply import scanned pictures of the cars.
- Use Movie Maker to create the project file crossroads.
- Adjust the duration of the pictures appropriately.
- Create the movie file crossroads.
- Play the animation a few times and see how you can improve it.
- If you need to improve the animation, you can only alter the project file and not the movie file.
- Make comments on whether the colours used are appropriate for your target audience.
- Make comments on the sequence of the pictures and suggest ways to improve the animation.

## Audio files

- Audio files such as MP3 (mp3), Windows (wav) and MIDI (midi) can be imported into the movie to enhance audio effect.
- You can search Internet sites, such as the Microsoft Office Online – Clip art and media homepage, to download free audio files.
- Alternatively, you can record the audio files yourself using any suitable software and hardware.
- Microsoft Windows 7 provides a simple recording tool to record sound in the Windows Media Audio File (.wma) format for up to 60 seconds.
- The only hardware you need is a microphone.
- Click , select ▶ **All Programs** , select ▌ **Accessories** and select ▌ **Sound Recorder** .
- Click ● Start Recording to start recording.
- Click ■ Stop Recording to stop recording.
- Save the recorded sound to the desired folder.
- To start a new recording, click ● Start Recording again.

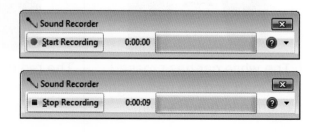

# Inserting audio files

- Inserting relevant audio files will make the animation more interesting.
- Click File and select Import into Collections... Ctrl+I.
- Import one or two audio files related to moving cars, such as sounding the horn.
- The audio files could be the sound you have recorded or suitable files downloaded from the Internet.
- On the bottom panel, click 🎬 Show Timeline to change it to the timeline mode.
- Drag and drop the audio files you have imported.
- Adjust the duration of the sound file in the same way that you adjust the duration of an individual picture.
- Play the animation.
- Do you think the audio files improve the quality of the animation and make it more interesting and appealing to the audience?
- Try different audio files to find the most suitable ones for the animation.
- Save the project file as cars.
- Create the movie file cars.

*These are the sound files. Do you think they are appropriate and make the animation more interesting?*

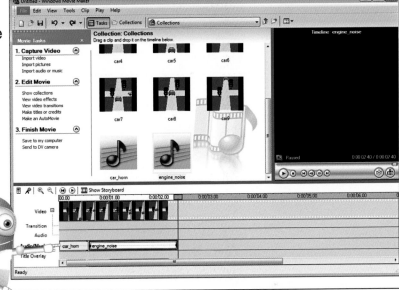

# Review 1

- Refer to your creation crossroads on the previous page.
- Assuming that your target audience are adult road users, explain how the animation you have created fits its purpose and is suitable for its target audience.

  Examples:
  o what is the purpose of the animation?
  o are the colours used appropriate?
  o are the pictures relevant and attractive?
  o have the pictures served their purpose?
  o is the music suitable for the purpose?
  o is the sequence and timing suitable?
  o has the animation made clear its purpose to the audience?

  (These are just some suggestions; you do not have to answer all the questions. At the same time, you can add any other comments you think appropriate and which indicate that you are aware how your animation can address your target audience.)

# Review 2

- Imagine that you want to present the same animation to a group of primary-school children who are not very familiar with traffic lights.
- Explain what you would change. Give reasons for any changes that you would make.
- Consider the colours, pictures and audio files. What improvements would you make so that the animation is more relevant and attractive to the young audience?

Answers for Review 1:

...................................................................................................................................

...................................................................................................................................

...................................................................................................................................

...................................................................................................................................

...................................................................................................................................

...................................................................................................................................

...................................................................................................................................

...................................................................................................................................

...................................................................................................................................

Answers for Review 2:

...................................................................................................................................

...................................................................................................................................

...................................................................................................................................

...................................................................................................................................

...................................................................................................................................

...................................................................................................................................

...................................................................................................................................

...................................................................................................................................

...................................................................................................................................

# 8.4 Video

## Planning

- Instead of using pictures to create an animation, students can use video clips to prepare a movie.
- The preparation is similar to that for animation.
- First, prepare a storyboard.
- Describe the series of video clips you will be preparing.
- Add in the duration for each video clip that you intend to capture.
- Include also the effect on the video clip, transition and caption that you may use.
- Be very clear who your target audience is and how you would make your video appropriate for your audience.

## A sample storyboard

- You have been working on a video project to promote a tourist attraction in your area – waterfall, to adult visitors, based on the following storyboard.

| Clip 1 |
| --- |
| Video clip or still photos showing the route leading to the site. |

| Clip 2 |
| --- |
| The source of the water. |

| Clip 3 |
| --- |
| The main scene — the great waterfall. |

| Clip 4 |
| --- |
| A close-up scene of the waterfall showing crystal clear water. |

| Video clip title | Duration (seconds) | Effect on video clip | Transition to next video clip | Caption (if used) |
| --- | --- | --- | --- | --- |
| Route | 16 | Fade out, To white | Bars | After crossing the bridge, the magnificent waterfall is just a few metres away! |
| Source of water | 13 | None | Checkerboard, Across | The source of the water comes from a height of more than 1000 metres. |
| The great fall | 16 | None | Dissolve | The height of the fall is 30 metres! |
| Close-up | 10 | None | Fade | Crystal clear water! |

### Shooting the clips

- You can shoot the actual scene by using a digital camera or a video camera.
- The format of the video clip depends on the type of camera and software that you use to process your video clips.
- Make sure you use a format that is supported by the software you will be using to produce the movie.
- If you are using Microsoft Movie Maker, it supports the following video files: .asf, .avi, .m1v, .mp2, .mp2v, .mpe, .mpeg, .mpg, .mpv2, .wm and .wmv.
- However, if your video files are not in the list above, there are many types of software available for converting them to one of the above supported formats.
- For exercise purposes, try to use the mpg, mpeg or wmv format.
- The avi format may give high quality output but the movie file produced will be very much bigger. It also uses a lot of RAM.
- Make sure you have enough hard-disk space (4 GB or more) and RAM (at least 512 MB) before you process the video and do the final movie. Insufficient memory will slow down your computer or even cause your computer to stop functioning normally, so you will not be able to complete the task of making the final movie.

### Tripod

- A tripod is a very useful accessory for capturing video.
- A tripod will help to keep the video camera still and thus prevent your recorded video from being jittery.
- A remote-control tripod lets you control the camcorder without having to press buttons on the camera itself; you are less likely to jiggle the camera as you start or stop the recording, or operate the zoom lens.
- This can be a real help in achieving smooth, professional-looking pans and tilts (when you capture a moving object by following it or by slanting the camera at an angle).
- It also improves the overall quality of the recorded video.

### Tips to improve quality of video

- Always use a still background when recording video.
- If you need to record against a moving background, try reducing the depth of field.
- You can also make the background go out of focus by using a lower level of light and by moving the subject closer to, or further away from, the lens.
- You can zoom in or take more close-up shots to avoid the moving background.
- You must provide adequate lighting; use soft light, diffuse (evenly distributed light) and consistent light levels.
- Avoid direct high-contrast lighting.
- If possible, the colours of the clothing that your subjects wear should complement their skin tone and be sufficiently different from the background or overlapping objects.
- Avoid bright colours, which tend to bleed or spread outside an object.
- Avoid stripes; these often create wavelike patterns, especially when the subject is moving slowly.

## Importing video clips

- Click **File**, select ☐ New Project    Ctrl+N .
- Click **File** and select Import into Collections... Ctrl+I .
- Select route.mpg and click [ Import ] to import the video clip into the collection pane.
- Repeat the process to import source of water.mpg, The great fall.mpg and close-up.mpg into the same collection.
- Click (▶) on top of the storyboard to render the movie.

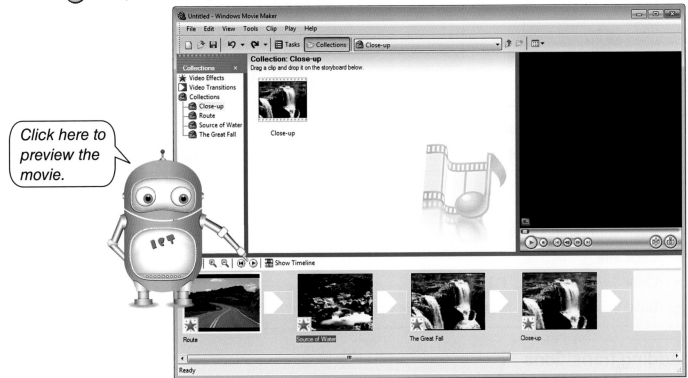

*Click here to preview the movie.*

## Video effects

- Use the video effect provided to add special effects to your movie.
- A video effect is applied for the entire duration that the video clip displays in your movie.
- You can add any of the video effects that appear in the Video Effects folder in the collections pane.
- Click **Tools**, select 📖 Video Effects to display the Video Effects folder.
- Select the video effect that you would like to include in the video clip that you have imported, by dragging it into the video clip on the storyboard.
- Click (▶) on the storyboard menu bar to render the movie to preview the effect.

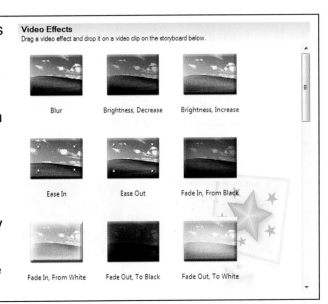

## Removing the effect

- If you have just added the video effect, you can remove it by clicking the undo button, ↩ or click `Edit` and select ↩ Undo Add Effect   Ctrl+Z .
- You may also right-click on the clip on the storyboard, select ★ Video Effects to obtain the following dialog table:

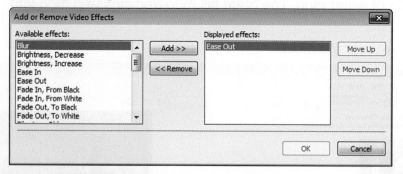

- Click `<< Remove` to remove the displayed effects.
- Or pick from the list of available effects and click `Add >>` to add the effect.

## Saving the project

- Save your project before you proceed.
- Click `File`.
- Click `Save Project As...   F12` .
- Save your project as *Your Name* movie project.

## Adding transitions

- Transitions control how the movie plays from one video clip to the next.
- You can add a transition between any two video clips on the storyboard.
- The transition will start to play before one clip ends and while the other clip starts to play.
- If no transition is added, there will a straight cut between the two clips.
- The transition that you have added will appear on the transition track of the timeline.
- You must expand the Video track if you want to view the track.
- To add a transition, click `Tools` and select 🎬 Video Transitions to open the Video Transitions folder in the collection pane.
- Choose the transition, drag and drop it between two clips on the storyboard.

Video transition inserted

## Editing the duration of transitions

- Insert two more transition styles.
- Click ▶ to preview the effect of the transitions.
- If you want to remove a transition, click on the transition and tap the delete key Delete .
- Click 💾 to save the project using the same filename before you proceed. You can change the duration of a transition.
- On the Transition track of the timeline, drag the beginning of the transition towards the beginning of the timeline to increase the transition duration.
- Drag the beginning of the transition towards the end of the timeline to decrease the transition duration.

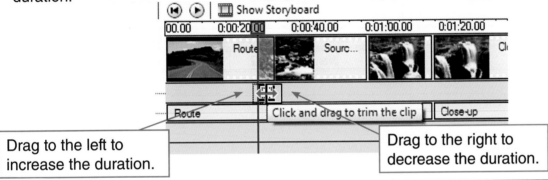

Drag to the left to increase the duration.

Drag to the right to decrease the duration.

## Background audio files

- Since we are showing a waterfall, if we can add some sound effects related to a waterfall, the movie created will be more realistic and attractive. This will also help to fulfil our aim of promoting the tourist site to our audience.
- To import the music files, click File.
- Click Import into Collections... Ctrl+I .
- You can import your own files or use the music files provided: water1.wma, water2.aif and water3.wma.
- Drag water1.wma to the Audio/Music track.
- Position the left side so that it aligns vertically with the left margin of the video clip source of water.wmv.
- As the music is too short, add another copy of water1.wma and position the two music clips side by side.
- Drag the right border of the second music clip to reduce its length as illustrated below:

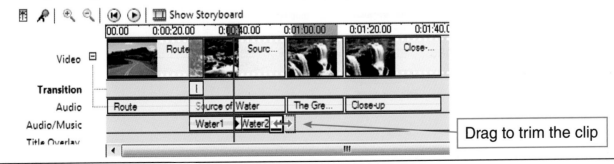

Drag to trim the clip

## More music

- Similarly, insert two copies of water2.aif and two copies of water3.wma.
- Adjust the duration to synchronise with the length of the video clips, The great fall.wmv and close-up.wmv, respectively.
- Render the entire movie to check the effect.
- Save the project as movie project with music.

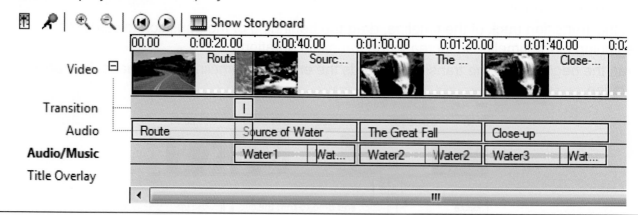

## Narrating the timeline

- You can enhance your movie by capturing an audio narration which lets you describe, in your own words and voice, what is displayed in the video.
- Before you can begin capturing an audio narration:
  - The playback indicator on the timeline must be at a position where the Audio/Music track is empty.
  - You must be in the timeline view.
- Click 🎤 on the storyboard/timeline menu bar to display the narration option.
- Prepare what you want to describe about the movie.
- Select Microphone as the audio input source.
- Check the Mute speakers option to avoid recording the background music.
- Click Start Narration to start recording.
- Click Stop Narration to end the recording.
- Save your recording as *Your name* narration.
- You may need to try a few times to adjust to the right timing.
- Render the movie.
- Save your project as movie with narration.

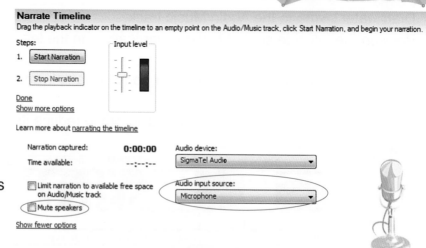

## Narration with background music

- You can capture your narration without muting the speakers, so that the background music will be recorded.
- After you have done the narration, check the track for music in the storyboard pane. You will find that the positions of the background music will be pushed to the right.
- Since the background music has been recorded, you can remove them from the music track.
- Click ![save] to save the project using the same filename.

> The music clips are included in the narration and are no longer needed. Remove them.

## Titles and credits

- To further enhance your movie, you can add titles and credits manually.
- Click Tools , select Titles and Credits... .
- You are given five options, pick one and click on the hyperlink to proceed.

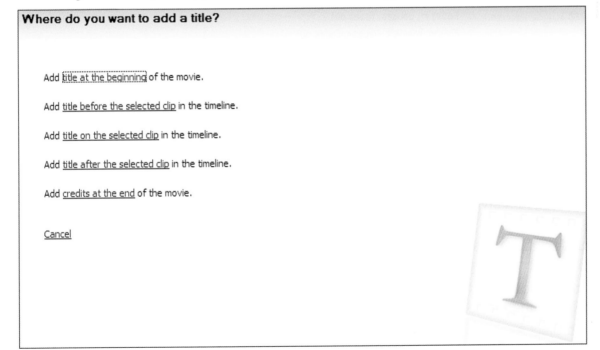

Where do you want to add a title?

Add title at the beginning of the movie.

Add title before the selected clip in the timeline.

Add title on the selected clip in the timeline.

Add title after the selected clip in the timeline.

Add credits at the end of the movie.

Cancel

## Title at the beginning

- Click at <u>title at the beginning</u>.
- Type the title Welcome to the great Kuching waterfall.
- As you type, you can see a preview on the right-hand side.

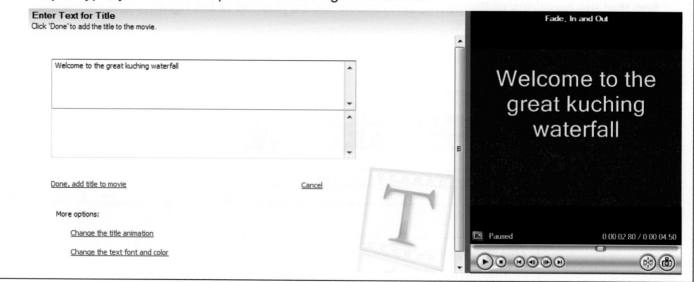

## Change the title animation

- Click <u>Change the title animation</u>.
- Select from the list for a suitable animation.
- Watch the preview on the right-hand side as you scroll up and down.

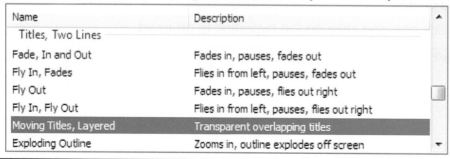

## Change the text font and colour

- Click <u>Change the text font and color</u>.
- Choose the font, font style, font size, colour and position.
- Click <u>Done, add title to movie</u> to add the title to the movie at the beginning.
- This will automatically add a new frame at the beginning of the movie.
- Save your project as movie with title.

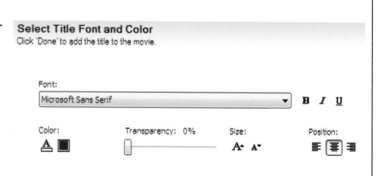

# 8.11 Other titles

## Title on the selected clip

- Let us add another title.
- Select the clip close-up.
- Select Add title on the selected clip in the timeline.
- Add the title as Crystal clear water!
- Click Change the title animation and select an appropriate animation.
- Click Change the text font and color.
- Choose the appropriate font, font style, font size, colour and position.
- Click Done, add title to movie to add the title to the clip selected.

## Credits at the end

- This is to add a new frame to record the credits of the movie.
- Use this to show your appreciation of those who have helped you in one way or another.
- Include your name and school and the date of creation.
- The layout for typing the text is slightly different.
- Watch the preview for the animation, font, font style, etc. on the right-hand side.

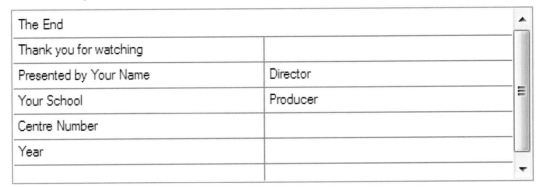

| The End | |
| --- | --- |
| Thank you for watching | |
| Presented by Your Name | Director |
| Your School | Producer |
| Centre Number | |
| Year | |
| | |

- You can also click Change the text font and color to choose the appropriate font, font style, font size, colour and position.
- Click Change the title animation and select an appropriate animation from the list under Credits.

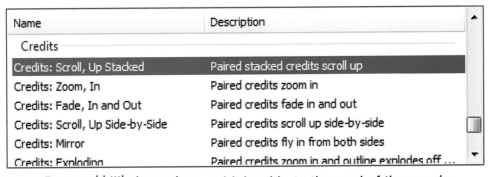

| Name | Description |
| --- | --- |
| Credits | |
| Credits: Scroll, Up Stacked | Paired stacked credits scroll up |
| Credits: Zoom, In | Paired credits zoom in |
| Credits: Fade, In and Out | Paired credits fade in and out |
| Credits: Scroll, Up Side-by-Side | Paired credits scroll up side-by-side |
| Credits: Mirror | Paired credits fly in from both sides |
| Credits: Exploding | Paired credits zoom in and outline explodes off ... |

- Click Done, add title to movie to add the title to the end of the movie.
- Render the movie a few times.
- Show it to your teacher, your friends and discuss how you can improve your movie.
- Save your project as *Your Name* movie with titles and credits.

## Create the final movie

- So far we have been saving a project which can be opened and edited.
- If you save it as a movie, it cannot be edited.
- Should you find any mistakes, you will need to edit the project file and save it as a movie again.
- Click File.
- Select Save Movie File...      Ctrl+P.
- Select My computer Save your movie for playback on your computer. and click Next >.
- Enter the file name as *Your Name* waterfall movie in your own folder or any folder specified by your teacher.
- Click Next > to accept the recommended quality.
- Wait for a while for the saving to be completed.
- You have the option to play the movie immediately using your default video player.
- Uncheck the option if you wish to play it later on.

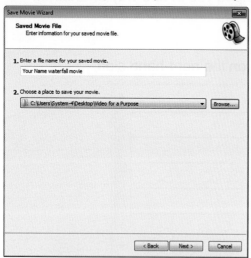

Type a filename and select a location to save the movie.

Click Next > to accept the recommended quality.

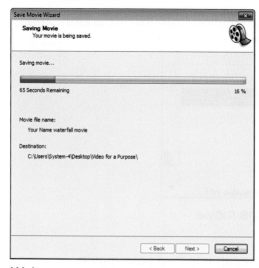

Wait...

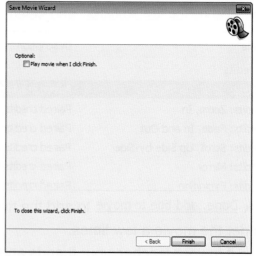

Clear the check box if you want to play the movie later.

## New project

- A friend from Vietnam wants to bring his parents to visit you next month. He has requested you to make a short movie of your home town. His parents are very keen to preview some of the tourist attractions, especially those connected with the costumes and culture of the local people.
- Use the following boxes to plan a storyboard of at least 4 scenes and prepare your video clips based on your storyboard.

| Scene 1 | Scene 2 |
|---------|---------|
|         |         |

| Scene 3 | Scene 4 |
|---------|---------|
|         |         |

## Planning the movie

- Use the table below to plan your final video or movie.

| Video clip title | Time (seconds) | Video effects (if used) | Transition (if used) | Caption (if used) |
|---|---|---|---|---|
|  |  |  |  |  |
|  |  |  |  |  |
|  |  |  |  |  |
|  |  |  |  |  |
|  |  |  |  |  |
|  |  |  |  |  |
|  |  |  |  |  |
|  |  |  |  |  |
|  |  |  |  |  |
|  |  |  |  |  |

## Editing

- Load Windows Movie Maker or any appropriate software for editing and compiling your movie.
- Import the relevant video clips that you have captured.
- Apply the video effects, transitions and captions to your clips, according to your plan.
  Save your project as *Your Name* home town.

## Narration and caption

- You can either:
  - o  Add narration with your own voice and save the narration as *Your Name* ht narration or
  - o  Import any relevant music.
- Make sure that the length of your audio file is equivalent to the length of your overall movie from start to end.
- Add a title caption at the beginning of the movie.
- Add your name, school and the centre number at the end of the movie as credits.
- Save your project as *Your Name* ht final.
- Save the complete movie as *Your name* ht final movie.

## Evaluation

- Explain your choice of video effects and transition and how these effects help to enhance the video to make it more interesting to your audience (your friend's parents).

......................................................................................................................................

......................................................................................................................................

......................................................................................................................................

......................................................................................................................................

- Explain how your audio file helps to enhance the video and make it more interesting to your audience (your friend's parents).

......................................................................................................................................

......................................................................................................................................

......................................................................................................................................

......................................................................................................................................

# Optional extension and challenge activities

## Module 8 – Video or Animation for a Purpose

### Challenge 1

- Plan a video or animation to show a rocket lifting off into space.
- Use a paper storyboard to help you plan.
- Add sound effects to improve the video.

### Challenge 2

Create source material for video or animation.

- Use a video camera to record a friend making a paper dart and flying it. Use close up and distance shots.
- Link the video clips into a short film.
- Edit any poor shots.
- Add a voice over and captions to explain how the dart is made.
- Add a title screen and credits.

# Optional extension and challenge activities

## Challenge 3

- Take video clips of your friends explaining why they like a particular pop star. Show them dancing to the music.
- Link the edited video clips into a short film.
- Add relevant music.
- Add a page of facts about the pop star with moving graphics, such as a beating drum.
- Use transitions to add interest.
- Add a title screen and credits.
- Evaluate your work.